RAILWAYS OF THE BRITISH EMPIRE

AFRICA

COLIN ALEXANDER &
ALON SITON

AMBERLEY

First published 2023

Amberley Publishing
The Hill, Stroud
Gloucestershire, GL5 4EP

www.amberley-books.com

Copyright © Colin Alexander & Alon Siton, 2023

The right of Colin Alexander & Alon Siton to
be identified as the Authors of this work has
been asserted in accordance with the Copyrights,
Designs and Patents Act 1988.

ISBN 978 1 3981 0790 8 (print)
ISBN 978 1 3981 0791 5 (ebook)

British Library Cataloguing in Publication Data.
A catalogue record for this book is available from
the British Library.

Typesetting by Hurix Digital, India.
Printed in the UK.

INTRODUCTION

Britain's global expansion began in the Middle Ages. However, although British merchant ships were regularly used in the lucrative West African slave trade as early as the sixteenth century, it was not until the late Victorian era that Britain's power and influence spread across continental Africa. The Slave Trade Act of 1807 heralded a new era in which the Royal Navy stopped slave ships, raided slave traders and negotiated with other European countries to combat slavery and, as much as possible, eradicate it.

This enlightened approach did much to improve British relationships with many parts of West Africa, which by the 1880s was dominated by Britain. British merchants imported precious metals and luxury goods from several African nations, which in turn were helped by their British allies to fight local wars. Tribal chieftains were allowed to rule by their own customs, but they paid taxes to Britain.

Sierra Leone had been established in 1787 as a colony for freed slaves, becoming in 1807 a British possession, along with The Gambia. These two territories would later merge with the Gold Coast to form British West Africa. The Cape Colony, later part of South Africa, followed in 1814.

Africa's first railway was established in 1852 in Alexandria, Egypt, long before British rule there, but had a great deal of British involvement in its construction. Across Africa, it was invariably the European colonial powers that built the majority of the continent's rail network. This was achieved at a huge price and with a terrifying death toll.

Railway construction in the south, meanwhile, commenced in 1859 when work began to connect Cape Town to nearby Wellington. Before this was completed, however, the first train had operated on a 2-mile stretch of line in Durban, in 1860.

1870 saw the arrival in Africa of Cecil Rhodes, a British entrepreneur who grew a near-monopoly in diamond mining in South Africa, where he became a politician. He envisaged a British-built Cape to Cairo railway to spread trade, investment and 'civilisation' throughout the continent. This ambitious route was first propounded by newspaper editor Edwin Arnold in 1874, catching the imagination of Cecil Rhodes. Sadly, his dream would never be realised in full.

Rhodes was instrumental in securing for the Empire the southernmost colonies of Africa, and his Cape to Cairo railway was intended to unify the continuous south to north red swathe of British possessions. As with the British-financed railways of the Indian subcontinent, it would enable swift deployment of the military to 'hot spots', and expedite the shipment of goods to African ports en route to Britain.

Its construction would be a major strategic challenge, for in a real-life game of *Blockbusters*, British attempts to build the north to south railway could only succeed if the ambitions of rival European powers were overcome. The French had designs on an east to west route, and the Portuguese had their own schemes, too. Crucially, in 1891, Germany secured vital territory in East Africa, which together with the taking of the Congo by Belgium put an end to Rhodes' plan.

That, however, was not the end of the Cape to Cairo story. In 1916, Allied forces took Tanganyika, part of German East Africa, finally securing the continuous sweep of 'red' colonies on the map. Britain at last had the territory it needed to build the Cape to Cairo Railway. The interwar economic Depression, however, prevented its progress and after the Second World War, the momentum was firmly behind independence for Africa's nations and the rationale for the project ceased to exist.

The sections that were built include one of the most spectacular feats of railway engineering anywhere in the world, the Victoria Falls Bridge. Cecil Rhodes said, 'Let the spray from the falling Zambezi River fall on the trains as they pass.' When the bridge opened in 1905 it was the highest in the world, its 650-foot span carrying it 420 feet above water.

Twelve years after Rhodes arrived in Africa, Britain seized power in Egypt and in neighbouring Sudan in 1899. This was to control the vital trade route through the 1869-built Suez Canal to India. The British military campaign in Sudan under Kitchener advanced along the Nile very gradually, not least because they built the railway as they progressed. They made a good job of it, for it forms part of Sudan's main line today, more than a century after it was built by the British army.

Echoing the early dominance of the East India Company in that subcontinent, it was British commercial enterprises that exerted control over much of Africa in the second half of the nineteenth century. The Royal Niger Company extended British influence in Nigeria, and the Gold Coast also became a British possession. The Imperial British East Africa Company took over what are now Kenya and Uganda, and the British South Africa Company operated in Rhodesia, now Zimbabwe and Zambia, and Nyasaland (Malawi).

During the Boer War in South Africa, both sides realised the strategic advantages of a railway network, and while the British used it for transport, the Boers employed guerrilla tactics, sabotaging bridges and infrastructure.

Following victory in South Africa, Britain annexed the Transvaal and the Orange Free State in 1902, which would be joined by Natal and the Cape Colony to form the Union of South Africa in 1910.

By 1900, the British Empire covered almost a quarter of the world's territories and more than a quarter of its population. As in India, British rule had a huge impact on the lives of millions of Africans.

It is difficult to make a judgement about British (and other European) rule in Africa. European influences compromised traditional cultures and permanently changed local economies, making them reliant on trade with Europe.

The British in particular invested in infrastructure, not only railways but also roads, telegraph cables, canals, irrigation systems and public utilities. This was no act of philanthropy towards the African people, but was instead to serve British interests in trade, defence and colonial government. A glance at Africa's railway map reveals the intent, showing how the main lines were built to transport extracted resources from Africa's interior to her ports, destined for European factories and markets.

Africa's railways also lured intrepid white settlers into thinly populated areas to cultivate the land and make profits. The territories of South Africa, Rhodesia and Kenya sought to increase their white populations through railway building.

There were disadvantages to Africa's improved communication with the rest of the world. After the First World War, a deadly flu epidemic was unknowingly carried along Africa's railway corridors by soldiers returning from the conflict, spreading the disease across the continent.

The advent of Africa's colonial railways brought about economic and demographic change. Where a long-distance line was projected connecting two points of worth, but passing through areas of little population or importance, the cheapest possible route would be selected. An example of this is the Uganda Railway, built between 1896 and 1901 to connect prosperous Uganda to the Indian Ocean. Germany had been a threat to British interests in East Africa, and the British government thought it essential that a rail link was forged from the port of Mombasa to the landlocked territory, rich in mineral wealth as well as being the source of the Nile.

A route was chosen through Kenya that kept construction costs to a minimum, but progress was hampered throughout. British investors were reluctant to put money into a scheme when the benefits were unclear. The terrain itself presented a major challenge to the experienced railway labourers shipped from British-ruled India and employed under primitive conditions. They had to deal with everything from tribal resistance to man-eating lions. There is a story that a stationmaster in Uganda sent a telegraph message reading, 'Lions eating clerk in booking office – kindly advise.'

The railway bypassed highly populated areas on its way from Mombasa to Kisumu on Lake Victoria. This led to the sparsely settled Kenyan land surrounding the railway being offered to European settlers, and the cultivation of coffee and tea expanded alongside the Kenya Uganda Railway, as did the population. In fact Edward Grigg described the KUR as the 'beginning of all history in Kenya' and said, 'it is the railway which created Kenya as a Colony of the Crown'.

Across Africa, railways decreased transportation costs, suddenly making exports profitable. A typical result of this was that by 1911, the Gold Coast was the world's largest exporter of cocoa. As in Kenya, there was a population explosion along the railway corridors and villages became cities.

Over a hundred years later, the locations that were served by the old railways are more developed and wealthy than non-railway cities of similar sizes, and feature better non-railway infrastructure such as hospitals and schools, which were built as part of the colonial legacy.

Following the Second World War, Britain's sphere of command in Africa actually grew in size, temporarily at least. This arose because Italy was stripped of most of her former empire by the newly formed United Nations.

Another post-war development was the Labour victory of 1945, a government which was sympathetic to calls for independence and liberation movements. The first major manifestation of this was the granting of India's independence in 1947, which immediately altered Britain's rationale for involvement in the Suez Canal. This was the beginning of the end of the Empire.

A year after India's independence and partitioning, South Africa elected a so-called Nationalist government, but one which was infamously committed to racial apartheid.

The pleas for independence of many African colonies were unsuccessful as the British government deemed them not sufficiently developed to be able to support themselves.

Next to fly the imperial nest was the stable and mature Gold Coast colony, an obvious candidate for the independence experiment, which emerged as Ghana in 1957. The tangible gratitude of the new Ghanaian population accelerated Britain's commitment to decolonisation, and the promise of independence was a major factor in the ending of Kenya's notorious Mau Mau rebellion.

The British Commonwealth survives as the symbolic descendant of the Empire, and the fact that Mozambique, without any historic British connection, joined the Commonwealth, demonstrates that Britain's legacy on the continent was not all negative.

Perhaps Britain's colonial legacy was expressed most eloquently by Nigeria's first Prime Minister, Sir Abubakar Tafawa Balewa, in his independence speech: 'We are grateful to the British officers whom we have known first as masters, and then as leaders, and finally as partners; but always as friends.'

Interestingly, in 2020, there is talk of a partnership between Hitachi and JK Minerals to reinvestigate the potential for a modern Cape to Cairo railway. Cecil Rhodes' dream may yet be realised. A positive part of his legacy is the European-financed railway network that connects modern Africa.

The sequence of illustrations begins in Egypt, as did Africa's railways, then we travel south and approximately clockwise around the continent through the various former British colonies, ending in the west in Sierra Leone. Although Gambia, further west again, was also part of the Empire, it had no railways.

I must here acknowledge the input of my friend Alon Siton, without whom this book would not be possible. All of the images reproduced here, with two exceptions, are from his collection. Thanks also to britishempire.co.uk and the excellent Grace's Guide website for some of the information.

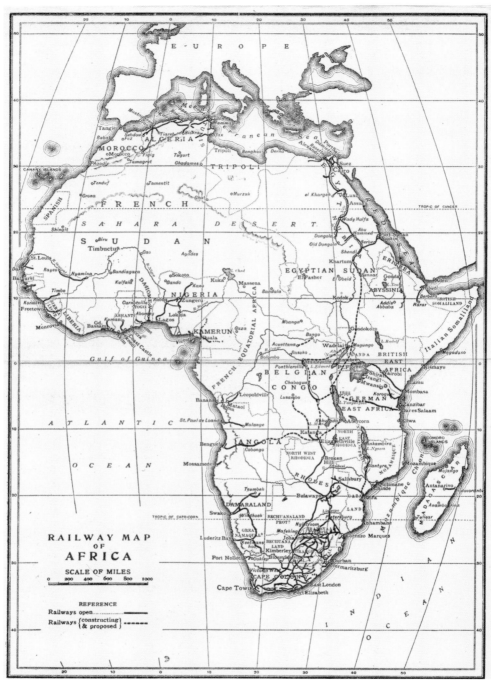

A comparison between this early African railway map and the next one showing the continent's colonies in colour, illustrates clearly how most of the first railways were concentrated in those territories controlled by Europe, and in particular those of the British Empire. Some of the projected lines shown would never be completed. (Alon Siton collection)

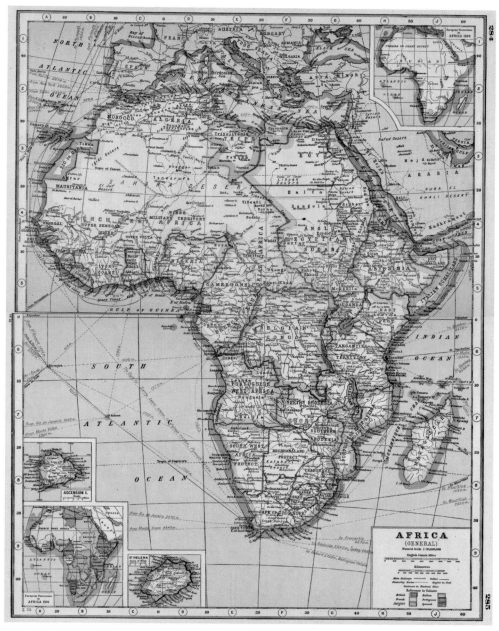

On this map dating from the interwar years, the swathe of pink stretching north to south, along with the separate colonies in the west, denotes the extent of the British Empire in Africa. Compare the corner inset maps: top right showing European territory in Africa in 1884, and bottom left just thirty years later. This frantic period of colonisation was known as the 'Scramble for Africa'. (Alon Siton collection)

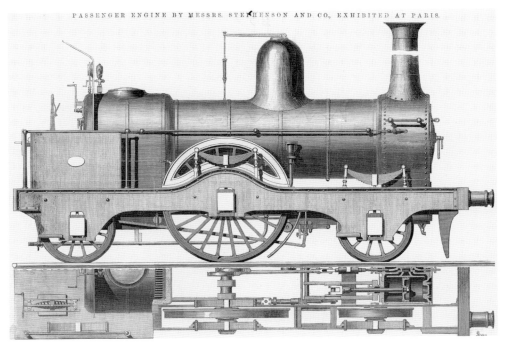

PASSENGER ENGINE BY MESSRS. STEPHENSON AND CO., EXHIBITED AT PARIS.

It was in Egypt that the first African permanent way was laid, and Britain's manufacturing industry supplied the necessary equipment. This 1867 illustration by John Swain from *The Engineer* shows a very British-looking 2-2-2 built by Robert Stephenson & Co. in Newcastle for the Egyptian Railway Administration. She was one of fourteen such engines built from 1858, and was shown at the Paris exhibition. (Alon Siton collection)

Robert Stephenson's connection with the Pasha, or Khedive of Egypt, led to prestigious orders for some of the most ornate locomotives ever. Three were built in the late 1850s and early 1860s, each with a luxurious saloon mounted behind the footplate. The Pasha was delighted with his purchase, and enjoyed driving it himself. (Alon Siton collection)

The Luxor to Aswan Railway was built to the narrower gauge of 3 feet 6 inches. This little 0-4-2, No. 15, was built for the LAR by Neilson of Glasgow in 1896. Seven years later this company would merge with two other Glaswegian firms, Dübs & Co. and Sharp Stewart, to form the giant North British Locomotive Company Ltd, which would go on to supply many of Africa's railways. (Alon Siton collection)

This Egyptian State Railways 0-6-0T, No. 506, was another Tyneside-built product of Robert Stephenson's. She typifies the British Victorian tank locomotive and is very similar to engines supplied by the same factory for the domestic market, such as 1891-built *TWIZELL* for Beamish Colliery, and is now preserved on the Tanfield Railway. (Alon Siton collection)

The aforementioned North British Locomotive Co. of Glasgow built a class of fifteen handsome 4-4-0 locomotives for the Egyptian State Railways. No. 694 is seen here in an official 1905 workshop portrait. They were long-lasting machines and their ornate footplate canopies would later be replaced by a more substantial cab. (Alon Siton collection)

This charming 1926 photograph shows a more modern-looking Egyptian 4-4-0, No. 201, with her crew proudly posing in the desert sand. She was rebuilt from a 4-4-2T by NBL in Glasgow in 1905. Note the delightful pair of six-wheeled coaches behind. (Alon Siton collection)

A vintage image of Egyptian State Railways No. 30 *KHEDIVE ISMAIL*, showing not only how locomotives were increasing in size and power output, but also the advances in the design of passenger stock. The 4-4-2 was one of a batch built by North British in 1925. Others of the same type were built in France, the USA and Germany, to the specification of J. M. E. Langton. (Alon Siton collection)

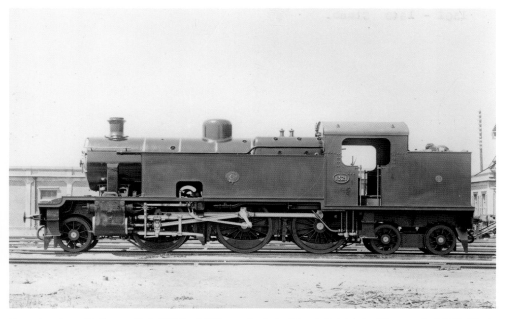

Egyptian State Railways 2-6-4T No. 1321 was built by North British in Glasgow in 1930. She is a typical modern suburban passenger tank locomotive of the era, and several of this design were built in Britain and Italy for service in Egypt. (Alon Siton collection)

A second glance at this locomotive reveals an unusual feature, which is a total lack of outside motion. The blowing of desert sand onto greasy slide-bars and piston rods was a constant maintenance headache for Egyptian State Railways. In a collaboration between North British and Sentinel, four of these geared, steam-motor locomotives were built 1937 with four axles, the middle two of which were driven separately. They were evidently not a success, however, as no more were built. (Alon Siton collection)

Much of the world's railway infrastructure and equipment was in major need of replacement after the Second World War. This 1947 glimpse inside Glasgow's Hyde Park works of the North British Locomotive Co. shows production in full swing. The 4-6-0s under construction are bound for the Egyptian State Railways. (Alon Siton collection)

A year later, one of the next batch of the same type of locomotive was captured in mid-air at Finnieston Quay, a short distance along the Clyde from the NBL works. This is Egyptian State Railways 4-6-0 No. 325 being craned into the hold of a cargo vessel, bound for Alexandria. The 2-8-2 on the left is yet another NBL export, No. 125 *RIVER OSHUN* headed for Nigeria. (Alon Siton collection)

North British may have dominated the export market for steam, but when it came to modern traction it was English Electric of Vulcan Foundry that led the way. EE was responsible for some of the first large diesel locomotives outside North America. Fresh out of Vulcan Foundry is No. 3009, one of twelve 1,600 hp diesel-electrics built in 1948 for Egypt, with the unusual wheel arrangement of 1A-Do-A1. This denotes four powered axles on the central rigid wheelbase and an articulated bogie at each end, with one powered and one trailing axle. (Alon Siton collection)

We could not leave Egypt without visiting the reason for Britain's presence there. A crew member on board a ship in the Suez Canal surveys the scene as a British-built Robinson ROD 2-8-0 hauls freight, tender-first, in the 1950s. Hundreds of these workhorses were supplied to the Railway Operating Department in the First World War for military service, and many remained overseas, some as far afield as Australia. (Alon Siton collection)

Moving south into Sudan, here we have another superb John Swain illustration from *The Engineer*. It portrays Sudan Expeditionary Railway 2-6-2T *ENDEAVOUR*, built by Manning Wardle in Leeds in 1896. She and a sister locomotive were supplied for the construction of the line from Wadi Halfa, on the Egyptian border, towards Dongola, and the 130-mile railway was completed in three months. (Alon Siton collection)

Once Sudan had some railways to operate, there was a need for motive power to haul the long-distance trains. This is the only known photograph of Sudan Government Railway 4-4-0 *ARGIN*, named after a town on the Egyptian border, and seen here at Wadi Halfa in 1904. The locomotive is thought to have been built in Leeds by Kitson or Hunslet and assembled in Sudan. (Alon Siton collection)

This official North British works photograph shows an altogether more powerful locomotive, 4-6-0 No. 107, one of several built for the Sudan Government Railway from 1904. They were joined by others of the same design constructed in Manchester by Beyer Peacock & Co. (Alon Siton collection)

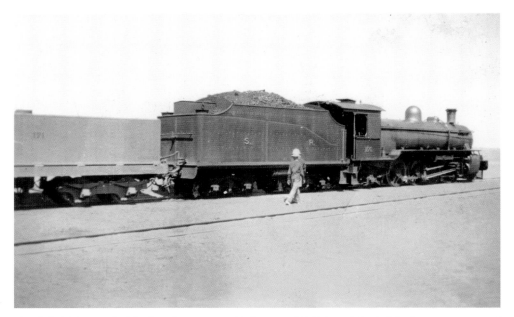

North British supplied Sudan Government Railways with lightweight 4-6-2s for passenger and 2-8-2s for freight. One of the latter, 1920-built No. 156, is seen here in a photograph probably taken in the 1930s, on a goods train. Note the white pith helmets for protection from the fierce desert sun, worn by the two men walking alongside the heavily loaded tender. (Alon Siton collection)

Powered by the same 350 hp English Electric unit that was installed in thousands of similar locomotives for Britain and beyond, Sudan Government Railways 0-6-0 diesel-electric No. 2 was built by R&W Hawthorn, Leslie & Co. in Newcastle in 1936. To British eyes accustomed to seeing such locomotives confined to shunting duties, it is a surprise to see No. 2 coupled to a passenger train. (Alon Siton collection)

Sudan Government Railways No. 509 was a modern 4-8-2, one of a class of forty-two built by North British in 1955. They had 4-foot 6-inch driving wheels for mixed-traffic use, and were the last steam locos operating in Sudan, lasting until the early 1980s. Among the many Sudanese people wandering on the track are a number of barefoot children. (Alon Siton collection)

This stylish vision of the future, 1950s-style, was one of the 1,850 hp Co-Co diesel-electric locomotives supplied by English Electric of Vulcan Foundry. The company, with a growing reputation at home and abroad for reliable diesels, supplied similar machines for railways in Australia and South America, as well as elsewhere in Africa. (Alon Siton collection)

SUDAN

1850 h.p. Co-Co 3′ 6″ gauge diesel-electric locomotives

Continuing south from Sudan, up the Nile and along what would have been Rhodes' Cairo to Cape route, we arrive in Uganda, promoted here to Europeans as a tourist destination. I wonder how the families of the Indian railway workers who were devoured by lions would have felt about this depiction? (Alon Siton collection)

Railway workers were not the only Indian import during the construction of the Uganda Railway. This was also true of motive power and rolling stock that had become surplus to requirements on the subcontinent. This is Class G No. 101, a pretty little 0-4-2, one of forty-five built in 1878 by Hawthorn's in Newcastle for the South Indian Railway. She moved to Uganda in 1897 during construction of the railway, where she remained the only one of her type. (Alon Siton collection)

Manchester-based Nasmyth Wilson & Co. was one of Britain's lesser-known locomotive builders. Nonetheless, by the 1930s well over 1,000 locomotives had emerged from its works, most of which were for export. They included a number of neat 2-6-2T and 2-6-4T engines for Uganda, and one of the latter, built in 1912, is shown here in this official photograph. (Alon Siton collection)

The major locomotive manufacturers produced illustrated catalogues to publicise their products in a burgeoning global marketplace. Vulcan Foundry was no exception and this page shows a Class EB3 4-8-0 for the Uganda Railway. No. 162, later East African Railways No. 2401, was built in 1922. She and her sisters were among the last operating steam locomotives in East Africa. (Alon Siton collection)

Freight vehicles, too, were exported from Britain. P&W MacLellan advertised this water-carrier for Uganda in an official 1925 book produced by the Gold Coast Railway for the Wembley British Empire Exhibition. This versatile Glasgow firm manufactured all kinds of structural steel products, including girders for the Forth Bridge. (Alon Siton collection)

This 1934 photograph shows white European passengers on board the Uganda Mail train at Nsinze. Between Mombasa and Kampala, the train passed through the undeveloped land from which Kenya was born. The line had been renamed the Kenya Uganda Railway in 1929, by which time traffic volumes necessitated much larger, more powerful locomotives. (Alon Siton collection)

The Manchester firm of Beyer Peacock provided the solution to the problem of moving increasingly heavy trains on lightly laid permanent way, over steep gradients and sinuous curves. This was the ingenious articulated Beyer Garratt, of which three are depicted here among other BP locomotives for export all around the world. Apart from the light axle loading, the Beyer Garratt design also obviated the need for costly double-heading and the extra manpower needed. (Alon Siton collection)

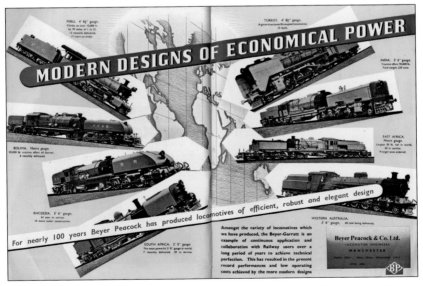

Five more Beyer Garratts appear here in another advertisement. Each one was effectively two locomotives supplied by a boiler suspended between them. One locomotive carried the water and the other the fuel. This arrangement permitted larger boilers and fireboxes, as there were no wheels directly beneath. The design was patented by Herbert William Garratt, who came to Beyer Peacock in 1907. (Alon Siton collection)

More than 1,600 Garratts operated worldwide, of which more than 1,100 came from Beyer Peacock, with other manufacturers building them under licence. An example of this is Kenya Uganda Railway Class EC2 4-8-2+2-8-4T No. 67 *BUSOGA*, one of ten built by North British in 1931. They lasted until about 1967, spending their final years in Tanzania. (Alon Siton collection)

Some of the Garratts were built for the British War Department, and this Kenya Uganda Railway Class EC4 4-8-2+2-8-4T carries her WD No. 74242 on her cab-side. She came from Beyer Peacock in 1945. This profile view illustrates the huge boiler diameter and the depth of the firebox. Like most KUR locomotives, she would be absorbed into the East African Railways fleet. (Alon Siton collection)

In 1948 when the railways of Tanganyika were amalgamated with the Kenya Uganda Railway, the system was named the East African Railways & Harbours Corporation, as seen on this map. Don Owens recalls that the resultant renumbering of locomotives caused difficulty for some of the local drivers, who took to tying coloured rags around handrails as an aid to recognition. (Alon Siton collection)

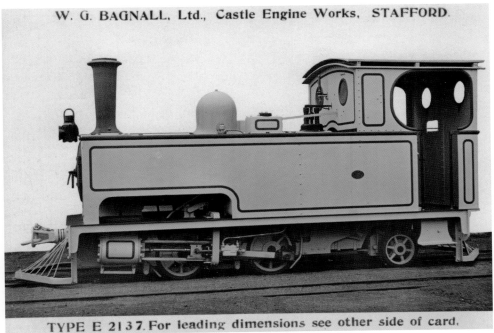

On the map above, the island of Zanzibar hugs the coast of what was then Tanganyika. Zanzibar had the first steam locomotives in East Africa, when Sultan Bargash built a short-lived private railway in 1879. Some years later another line was built from the Arab Fort in Zanzibar town to the village of Bububu. This Bagnall-built 0-4-2T arrived in 1920 to haul materials for harbour construction. (Alon Siton collection)

W. G. ⬤GNALL LTD., CASTLE ENGINE WORKS, S⬤FFORD

TYPE E.2675 FOR LEADING DIMENSIONS SEE OTHER SIDE OF CARD

Further out in the Indian Ocean, and once classed as part of Britain's East African territory, is the island of Mauritius. It had a railway network that was far more extensive than that on Zanzibar. At one time it even operated Beyer Garratts! Like the Zanzibar locomotive above, this 0-6-0T was built by Bagnall of Stafford, and was delivered to the island in 1942. (Alon Siton collection)

MAIL TRAIN - TANGANYIKA RAILWAYS, DAR-ES-SALAAM

Back on the mainland of Africa, this vintage postcard shows the Tanganyika Railway Mail Train crossing a stretch of fairly featureless grassland. The train ran between Dar es Salaam and Kigoma on the shore of Lake Tanganyika, and is seen here with a G Class 4-8-0, later East African Railways 22xx series, in charge. (Alon Siton collection)

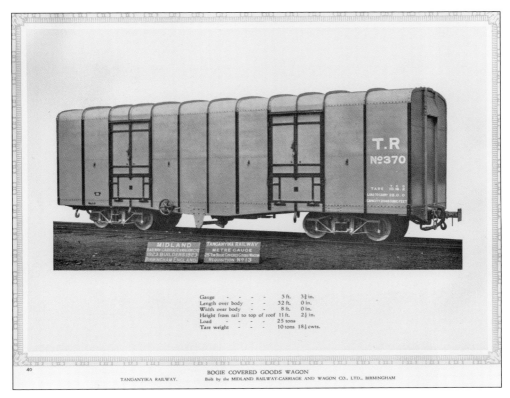

Cammell Laird was a large British engineering firm manufacturing everything from springs to ships. Its railway division would later form part of Metropolitan Cammell, and among its associate companies was the Midland Railway Carriage & Wagon Company of Birmingham. This catalogue shows a covered bogie 25-ton goods wagon for the metre-gauge Tanganyika Railway, built in 1923. (Alon Siton collection)

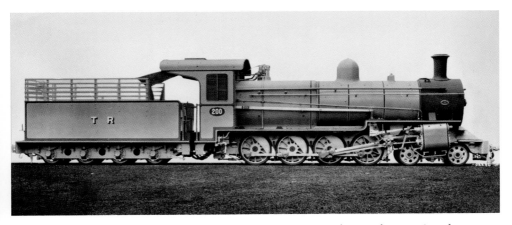

As well as the Garratts, Beyer Peacock built many conventional steam locomotives for export to the Empire. This is Tanganyika Railway Class DL No. 200, built at the Gorton Foundry in 1923. The 4-8-0 was almost unknown as a wheel arrangement in the UK, but was commonplace across Africa, especially on the metre-gauge systems. (Alon Siton collection)

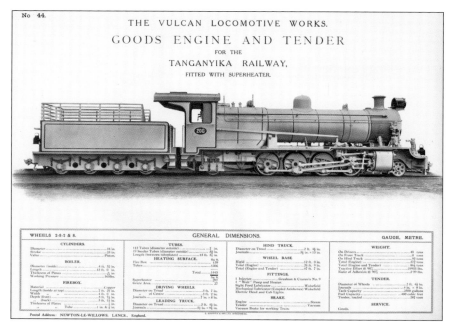

No 44.

THE VULCAN LOCOMOTIVE WORKS.

GOODS ENGINE AND TENDER

FOR THE

TANGANYIKA RAILWAY,

FITTED WITH SUPERHEATER.

WHEELS 2-8-2 & 8.	GENERAL DIMENSIONS.	GAUGE, METRE.

Postal Address: NEWTON-LE-WILLOWS, LANCS., England.

Of similar size and power output to the 4-8-0 above, but of a different arrangement, this 2-8-2 from Vulcan Foundry is, to my eyes, more aesthetically pleasing. She is Tanganyika Railway Class MK No. 206, which later became EAR No. 2501. She was one of eleven such locomotives built from 1925, and the design was developed into the similar ML Class. (Alon Siton collection)

In 1971, railway preservation was in its infancy in both Britain and Africa. EAR Class 10 2-6-4T No. 1003 was displayed on a short length of track in Jamhuri Park, Nairobi. These eight-tank engines were built by Nasmyth Wilson in 1913 and were due for scrapping in the late 1930s. The extra traffic generated by the Second World War gave them a reprieve and they then lasted in service until the 1960s. (Alon Siton collection)

East African Railways 4-8-0, No. 2429, formerly Kenya Uganda Railway No. 190, is seen here at Nairobi in 1979. She was built at Vulcan Foundry in 1925. A member of the Uganda Railway's Class GD, later reclassified EB3 on the KUR, and eventually EAR 24 Class, they were a larger, modified version of the earlier, experimental, UR GC Class. (Alon Siton collection)

Another of the Tanganyika Railways Class MK 2-8-2s, the former TR No. 213, was by the time of this photograph renumbered as East African Railways No. 407. She would later become Class 25 No. 2508 and was built at Vulcan Foundry, Newton-le-Willows in 1926. (Alon Siton collection)

Surely one of the most imposing metre-gauge locomotive types ever built was the Uganda Railway's EA Class 2-8-2? No. 2804 *KILIFI*, ex-Kenya–Uganda Railway No. 4 was one of six locomotives built at Robert Stephenson's Darlington works in 1928, and became East African Railways' Class 28. (Alon Siton collection)

Classmate of EAR No. 2429 seen above, No. 2462 was built not at Vulcan, but by Nasmyth Wilson in 1930. The former Kenya Uganda Railway No. 223 was photographed at Nairobi locomotive shed on 22 August 1971. The first GD Class 4-8-0s entered service on the Uganda Railway in 1923, and a total of sixty-two locomotives were built by the two manufacturers. (Alon Siton collection)

This is East African Railways Class 22 4-8-0 No. 2216, built by Nasmyth Wilson in 1930. Originally built for the Uganda Railway, they were then known as GB Class and later as EB1 on the Kenya Uganda Railway. Other 22s came from the Tanganyika Railway, and as well as Nasmyth Wilson, they were built by Robert Stephenson's and North British. (Alon Siton collection)

While perhaps not as glamorous as steam locomotives and rolling stock, signalling apparatus was another commodity exported from Britain to its imperial outposts. A notable manufacturer of such mechanical equipment was Saxby & Farmer, later part of Westinghouse. This mechanical ground frame at Nairobi West was photographed in 1971. (Alon Siton collection)

Another photograph taken on 22 August 1971, this is an overall view of Nairobi locomotive shed in Kenya. Nairobi was East African Railways' largest depot, and this quiet scene includes a Tribal Class, a pair of Beyer Garratts and a large tank locomotive. (Alon Siton collection)

Wickham of Ware in Hertfordshire was a manufacturer specialising in lightweight railcars powered by internal combustion engines. East African Railways Rail Car No. 3 was delivered to the Kenya Uganda Railway in May 1946, and was fitted with a Saurer engine. It was one of three such bogie railcars with seating for fifty-eight passengers. (Alon Siton collection)

This advertisement shows an East African Railways train made up of Metropolitan Cammell aluminium alloy coaching stock, and hauled by a Beyer Garratt. Even after the Second World War, British manufacturers continued to win valuable contracts for the supply of rolling stock for export around the world. (Alon Siton collection)

At Nairobi shed in 1969 is Garratt Class 58 4-8-4+4-8-4T No. 5813, built by Beyer Peacock in Manchester in 1949. Eighteen of them were ordered by the Kenya Uganda Railway following the Second World War, but by the time they entered service, the KUR had been absorbed by the East African Railways. Note the distinctive oblong Giesl ejector chimney. (Alon Siton collection)

Nakuru, north-west of Nairobi, is the location for this 1971 shot of another Class 58, No. 5812, also from Beyer Peacock in 1949. The articulated metre-gauge Garratts were the masters of East Africa's gradients. She is heading for Kisumu on the shore of Lake Victoria with a freight train. The antiquated water crane looks slightly incongruous with the modern station architecture. (Alon Siton collection)

In contrast to the mighty Beyer Garratts, this humble East African Railways Class 80 diesel shunter No. 8004 was built by Fowler in Leeds in 1950. One of six, she was powered by an 80 hp McLaren engine driving her coupled wheels via a mechanical transmission and jackshaft. I wonder if her youthful driver envied his colleagues on the Garratts? (Alon Siton collection)

This is an official 1951 works photograph of new North British 2-8-2 No. 2903 for East African Railways. She carried the name *BUNYORE*, after a community in the west of Kenya. Like the similar Class 31 2-8-4s, the Class 29s carried the names of tribes, and were sometimes known as the Tribal Class. They were based on the Nigerian River Class (q.v.). (Alon Siton collection)

After steam ended on British Railways in 1968, many railway photographers were lured overseas. This is Mombasa shed on 1 September 1971, with a party of enthusiasts in attendance. On the left is EAR Tribal Class 29 2-8-2 No. 2912 *KAKAMEGA*, built by North British in 1952. Beyond her, tucked inside the shed, is a Beyer Garratt, and another of these giants is on the right. (Alon Siton collection)

This 1971 view of Nairobi shed reveals EAR Class 13 No. 1311 awaiting overhaul. She was built as a 4-8-2T by North British in 1953. Designed for heavy shunting duties, they had a tendency to derail and lacked sufficient water capacity. Both problems were solved when they were rebuilt as 4-8-4Ts with larger tanks, taking their rear bogies from scrapped Garratts. (Alon Siton collection)

The twenty-nine members of EAR's Class 60 4-8-2+2-8-4T Garratt were ordered from Beyer Peacock, and the first twelve were subcontracted to Société Franco-Belge in France. The remainder were built in Manchester, including No. 6015 in 1954. They were named after governors, in this case *SIR ROBERT BROOKE POPHAM*, seen on freight duty in 1975, by which time her nameplates had been removed. (Alon Siton collection)

Similar to the Class 29s but of 2-8-4 wheel arrangement, this is EAR Class 31 No. 3146 *WAMIA*, built by Vulcan Foundry in 1955. The photograph was taken at Birkenhead West Dock, where she awaited shipping to Africa in March 1956. Note the U-shaped cross-section spokes on her SCOA-P driving wheels (patented by the Steel Company of Australia), a weight-reduction measure. (Alon Siton collection)

Seen in December 1970, the Mombasa–Nairobi freight train has paused at Miritini, 8 miles into its journey, behind EAR Class 59 4-8-2+2-8-4T No. 5931 *ULGURU MOUNTAINS*. The 59s were a class of thirty-four oil-fired metre-gauge Garratts, all named after East African mountains, and were built by Beyer Peacock in Manchester from 1955. (Alon Siton collection)

Sister locomotive No. 5909 *MOUNT MGAHINGA* rests between duties at Nairobi in 1969. The Class 59s were the largest, heaviest and most powerful steam locomotives on any metre-gauge railway in the world. They weighed 252 tons and developed a tractive effort of 73,500 lbs. Incidentally, the 76-ton breakdown crane towering over the Garratt was built by Ransomes & Rapier of Ipswich. (Alon Siton collection)

Photographed at Mombasa shed on 1 September 1971, this is EAR 2-8-2 No. 2921 *MASAI OF KENYA*, built by North British in Glasgow in 1955. She was one of the later batch of Class 29 locomotives with a larger smokebox door and can be seen today at Nairobi Railway Museum. (Alon Siton collection)

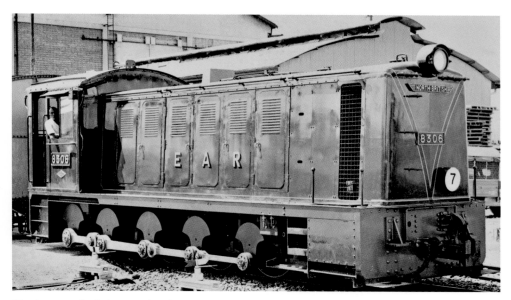

Having supplied thousands of steam locomotives to every continent, the excellent reputation of North British was tarnished by its essays in modern traction. One of the company's rare diesel successes was its 0-8-0 design for East African Railways, such as No. 8306 here. There were twenty-seven of them in total, powered by Paxman or MAN engines via a hydraulic torque-convertor and jackshaft drive. (Alon Siton collection)

Sagana was on a branch line from Nairobi, and it had its own small locomotive shed. A branch line shed in Britain might house a small tank or 0-6-0 locomotive, but they did things differently in Africa. On 3 September 1971, it was home to East African Railways Class 31 2-8-4 No. 3110 *BAKIGA*. She was built at Vulcan Foundry in 1955. (Alon Siton collection)

Sister locomotive No. 3132 *KUMAM* has stopped for water at Thika, north-east of Nairobi, in 1976. She is in charge of a lengthy freight train and her crew has allowed her tender tank to overflow. She was another 1955 product of Vulcan Foundry. Both water crane and water tower, visible above the fourth vehicle, would almost certainly have been shipped from Britain. (Alon Siton collection)

The 1950s and 1960s was a time when several British manufacturers built speculative diesel prototypes in the hope of winning orders. Clayton of Derbyshire built the *Explorer* in 1959, a Co-Co diesel-electric locomotive powered by a Lister Blackstone 1,100 hp 12-cylinder engine with AEI (British Thomson Houston) electrics. She was leased to East African Railways who later bought her outright, becoming the sole member of EAR's Class 79. (Alon Siton collection)

As in Egypt and Sudan, it was English Electric that won the bulk orders for East Africa's early main line diesel fleet. The 44 locomotives of Class 90 were delivered from 1960 onwards. No. 9023 is seen in pristine condition at Nairobi, and a look at her bogies reveals the 1Co-Co1 wheel arrangement. This denotes that each bogie had a traction motor on each of the inner three axles, and a pair of trailing wheels at the outer end. (Alon Siton collection)

Passing close to Nairobi's golf club, No. 9023 is seen again in charge of a freight train composed of modern-looking bogie wagons. These handsome products of Vulcan Foundry employed English Electric's reliable 12-cylinder 1,840 hp power unit. On the horizon can be seen the Nairobi Parliament Building. (Alon Siton collection)

At Nakuru, the single-line token is exchanged by the crew of EAR No. 9042 as she hauls a heavy freight in 1969. Everything about this image is charming, from the lower-quadrant semaphore signals and the breeze-block signal cabin to the flowerbeds beside it and the clean white suit of the signalman performing the exchange. (Alon Siton collection)

Situated about 70 miles east of Lake Victoria, and only 4 miles from the equator is the small town of Timboroa. At 9,001 feet above sea level, this is the highest railway station in the British Commonwealth, and this 1971 scene shows a passenger train calling there. Nearby is Timboroa Summit, which at 9,136 feet is the highest altitude of any railway in the former British Empire. (Alon Siton collection)

Having become Class 87, sister locomotive Nos 8740 (formerly 9040) and 8723 (9023) have had their elegant lined red livery replaced by a rainbow scheme. Despite the garish livery and powerful headlight, these heavy diesel-electrics were vulnerable to stray wildlife on the track. A collision with a giraffe or an elephant could dent the nose compartment, damaging air pipes and electrical conduit, and disabling the locomotive. (Geoff Cooke)

South of the former Tanganyika (now Tanzania) was the much smaller territory of Nyasaland which lies on the west shore of Lake Malawi. The very British-sounding Shire Highlands Railway was a private venture built to improve communication in the landlocked territory. 0-4-0ST No. 1 *THISTLE*, built by Bagnall of Stafford in 1903, was used in its construction. (Alon Siton collection)

The Shire Highlands Railway needed powerful locomotives to work freight trains over its gradients. 4-8-0 Class D No. 9, seen in this official portrait, was a 1914 product of Hawthorn Leslie in Newcastle. Others arrived later from North British. Engines of the same type were operated by the Central Africa Railways and the Trans-Zambezia Railway, also in Nyasaland. (Alon Siton collection)

This is Luchenza station in 1962, and Nyasaland Railways Class G 2-8-2 No. 37 *ROBERT LAWS* is receiving some attention from one of her crew, perhaps a drop of oil. She was built by North British in Glasgow in 1949 and is seen at the head of a mixed train with freight wagons marshalled in front of some modern-looking passenger stock. (Alon Siton collection)

In 1958, Nyasaland was celebrating the Silver Jubilee of its public railways. For the event, No. 1 *THISTLE* was lined up alongside Nyasaland Railways No. 57, another 2-8-2 newly arrived from North British. Happily, No. 1 is preserved at Limbe, and No. 57 is preserved at the Livingstone Railway Museum in Zambia. (Alon Siton collection)

Twenty Zambezi Class diesel-electrics with 1,200 hp Sulzer engines were ordered from Metro-Cammell in Birmingham for Nyasaland's Trans Zambezia Railway. A further thirty-three were built for Nigeria and Zambia. This is the first, No. 200, being craned onto the *CLAN MACLACHLAN* for export in 1963. A year later, Nyasaland was renamed Malawi. (Alon Siton collection)

THE CAPE TO CAIRO RAILWAY : A PLATELAYERS' ENGINE AT SALISBURY.

Nyasaland was bordered by Rhodesia, named after Cecil Rhodes. Its capital was Salisbury (now Harare in Zimbabwe) and this 1899 image, taken there, shows 'empire-builders' posed on a contractor's locomotive built by Fowler in Leeds in 1896. At this time, the 'Scramble for Africa' was in full swing, and the new railway was intended to connect the Cape to Cairo. (Alon Siton collection)

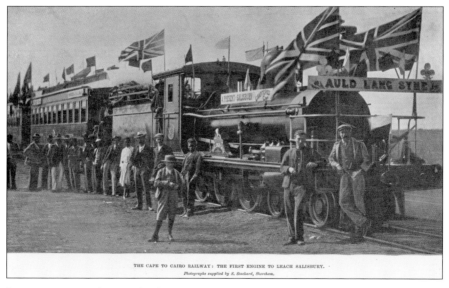

THE CAPE TO CAIRO RAILWAY : THE FIRST ENGINE TO REACH SALISBURY.
Photographs supplied by S. Stockard, Shoreham.

Another 1899 image depicts the first train to reach Salisbury, on the Mashonaland Railway. The Inauguration Special consisted of coaches originally built for Brazil's Sao Paolo Railway. Locomotive No. 2 *RALEIGH GREY* came from Neilson of Glasgow in 1882. She was named after a coloniser of Southern Rhodesia. The line was built to Cecil Rhodes' preferred gauge of 3 feet 6 inches, which was known as Cape Gauge. (Alon Siton collection)

The first railway in Southern Rhodesia (now Zimbabwe) was the Bechuanaland (Botswana) Railway, which reached Bulawayo on the border in 1897. The next stage crossed the mighty Zambezi River at the Victoria Falls in September 1905 on this spectacular bridge. Crossing the bridge brought trains into Northern Rhodesia, which is now Zambia. (Alon Siton collection)

Naturally, Rhodesia's original locomotive fleet was made in Great Britain. Rhodesia Railways' 10th Class 4-8-2 No. 98 was built by the North British Locomotive Co. in 1913. She is now preserved in Bulawayo. She is seen alongside another NBL product, 12th Class 4-8-2 No. 177, built in 1926. (Alon Siton collection)

Here is a sister locomotive of museum-piece No. 98 seen on the previous page, and this one is very much in revenue-earning service. This vintage view of the busy station at Bulawayo shows Rhodesia Railways' 10th Class 4-8-2 No. 98, built by North British in 1913, with a through train to Cape Town. (Alon Siton collection)

North British supplied a further series of 4-8-2s to Rhodesia in the mid-1920s. These were known as the 12th Class, of which No. 185 is seen here in steam. Sister engine No. 204 still operates in Zambia, taking tourists to Victoria Falls on the Zambezi Sawmills Railway. (Alon Siton collection)

At about the same time as the 12th Class 4-8-2s were being shipped from Scotland to Rhodesia, also heading in that direction from Manchester were the twelve members of the 13th Class. These 2-6-2+2-6-2T Garratts were built at Beyer Peacock and one is seen here curving past a small settlement with a freight train in the 1950s. (Alon Siton collection)

A detailed, broadside view of another of Rhodesian 12th Class in an official portrait. RR No. 190 was built by North British in 1926. As well as the usual diamond-shaped works plate on the smokebox, the additional plate on her cylinder identifies her as one of ten members of the class originally fitted with Lentz poppet valve gear. (Alon Siton collection)

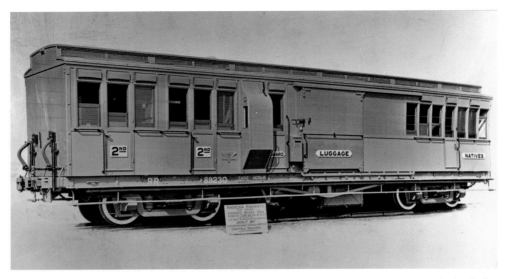

Compared to the 12th Class 4-8-2s, this clerestory-roofed brake composite coach, built for Rhodesian Railways by Cravens of Sheffield in 1929, looks positively archaic, not least in its attitude towards its occupants. Note the separate compartments for second class passengers and for 'natives'. (Alon Siton collection)

North British 1930-built No. 249, a Rhodesian Railways 12th Class, stands beneath the impressive control tower at Bulawayo station. Note the additional water-carrier marshalled behind the locomotive's tender. She later became the property of Zambia Railways. (Alon Siton collection)

In 1947 the royal family made its first post-war overseas state visit, taking in South Africa and Southern Rhodesia. Princess Elizabeth celebrated her twenty-first birthday during the tour, which included a stay at Victoria Falls and a visit to the grave of Cecil Rhodes. A newly built royal train was provided, hauled by a pair of Garratts in a deep blue livery, with a water tank between them, as seen in this Beyer Peacock publicity material. (Alon Siton collection)

The Royal Train in Rhodesia

The Garratts used on the royal train were members of the legendary 15th Class, one of only two types built with the 4-6-4+4-6-4T wheel arrangement. The only others were built for Sudan and they later moved to Rhodesia. In a more typical condition than the royal blue pair is No. 376 *INGULUNGUNDU*, seen here at Westgate shed, Bulawayo. She was built at Beyer Peacock's Gorton Foundry in 1948. (Alon Siton collection)

Rhodesia Railways' 15th Class met a requirement for a Garratt with larger diameter driving wheels for higher speeds, based on the Sudanese examples, with semi-streamlined front water tanks. They were supremely reliable and averaged 6,000 miles per month. This is No. 396 *IGOGO*, also at Westgate. She was built at Beyer Peacock in 1949. (Alon Siton collection)

The two work-stained Beyer Garratts seen at Westgate are in stark contrast to pristine No. 403, in workshop grey for photographic purposes outside Gorton Foundry in 1950 before delivery to Rhodesia. The first four were built in 1940, the remaining seventy following between 1947 and 1952, making them the second most numerous class of Garratts to be built. (Alon Siton collection)

At first glance you might mistake this locomotive for a 15th Class Beyer Garratt, but a closer look reveals the smaller-diameter eight-coupled wheels of a 2-8-2+2-8-2T. There were thirty members of Rhodesia Railways Class 16A, built at Beyer Peacock in 1952 and 1953. No. 621, seen here on a freight train, was second in the series. She was scrapped in Zambia in 1995. (Alon Siton collection)

Another Class 16A, No. 634, built in 1953 by Beyer Peacock, is the subject of this colour transparency taken in 1975. She is rumbling over an ungated rural level crossing as she approaches a passing loop. Later that year she went on loan to the Caminhos de Ferro de Moçambique, where she remained until 1981. (Alon Siton collection)

Rhodesia's Class 14A 2-6-2+2-6-2T was a smaller, lighter Garratt, based on the pre-war Class 14. No. 512 was one of eighteen built at Beyer Peacock in 1953 and 1954. They were described as free-running, and capable of 60 mph. Political sanctions on Rhodesia from 1975 saved them from the scrapyard, and they were refurbished with roller bearings. They eventually retired in 1993 and several survive in operation for tourist trains. (Alon Siton collection)

This fascinating 1954 view shows the boiler section of 20th Class Beyer Garratt 4-8-2+2-8-4T No. 704 en route from Manchester to the Mersey. They were fitted with mechanical stokers, and were the most powerful locomotives in Rhodesia, capable of hauling massive loads up steep gradients. Notice the British Railways 'cycling lion' emblem on the cab of the Pickfords tractor. (Alon Siton collection)

By the late 1950s, with independence sweeping the continent, fewer orders were being placed with British manufacturers and Africa's railways could look elsewhere. In 1957, however, the Gloucester Railway Carriage & Wagon Co. was still turning out vehicles for Rhodesia Railways, such as 4th Class coach No. 4127. (Alon Siton collection)

Crossing the border into South Africa, fifteen years had elapsed since the first train from Durban, by the time Beyer Peacock delivered ten diminutive 2-6-0s to the Cape Government Railways in 1875. Eight more came from Avonside in Bristol. Later to be designated 1st Class, four were sold to Sudan in 1884, and all were withdrawn by 1916. (Alon Siton collection)

4-6-0T No. 13 was one of seven built by Kitson of Leeds in 1879 for Natal Government Railways, where they were joined by another thirty from Robert Stephenson's. They were used on services out of Durban. In 1913, she was sold into industrial use with the Victoria Falls Power Co. Ltd. In 1979, she became the first locomotive in South Africa, and probably the world, to complete a century of continuous service, and is now preserved. (Alon Siton collection)

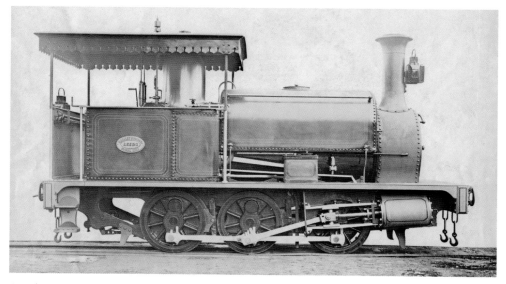

Another 1879 product of Leeds that saw service in Durban was this 0-6-0 saddle-tank, built by the Hunslet Engine Company for the South African Harbour Board. Other than her Egyptian-style canopy, she was typical of small, British industrial steam locomotives. (Alon Siton collection)

The Kimberley diamond rush of the 1870s was a major catalyst for railway construction in South Africa, as was the opening-up of the Witwatersrand goldfield in 1886. Judging by the tubs in the foreground, this scene appears to be near mineral workings. What is certain is that this precious silver gelatin image shows Cape Government Railways 5th Class 4-6-0 No. 123, built by Dübs & Co. in Glasgow in 1891. (Alon Siton collection)

This remarkable image captures the first train to arrive at St. Mark's in the Eastern Cape province of South Africa. The locomotive beneath the banner appears to be an ex-Cape Government Railways Class 7A 4-8-0, built by Neilson & Co. in 1892. Note the two motor cars on the left, fitted with flanged wheels for rail use. This dates the occasion to around the time of the First World War. (Alon Siton collection)

An illustration by the great John Swain for *The Engineer* magazine shows Cape Government Railways 7th Class 4-8-0 No. 340. She was built by Neilson of Glasgow in 1892. A total of thirty-nine of these locomotives came from Neilson and Dübs. Like all main line engines in South Africa, they were built to the 3-foot 6-inch Cape Gauge. (Alon Siton collection)

This 1898 scene depicts the aftermath of an accident at Mosterts Hook near Matjiesfontein on the Cape Government Railways. Matjiesfontein is 160 miles from Cape Town, and before dining cars were available, trains stopped here so that passengers could eat at nearby Logan's Hotel. Legend has it Logan's soup was so hot that the train whistle would summon passengers before they ever got to their main course! (Alon Siton collection)

Strangely, the term 6th Class applied to several locomotive types in South Africa, with many variations including three different wheel arrangements. Most were 4-6-0s, such as Cape Government Railways No. 375, built by Sharp Stewart of Glasgow in 1897. She was beautifully illustrated in *The Engineer* by John Swain. She eventually became No. 465 of South African Railways. (Alon Siton collection)

This glorious colour transparency shows South African Railways Class 6A 4-6-0 No. 462, built by Dübs in 1897, at De Aar, Northern Cape province. Originally Cape Government Railway No. 182, she sports a rather fetching copper chimney cap. She survives at the Big Hole Mining Museum at Kimberley. Notice also the self-propelled petrol railcar on the left. (Alon Siton collection)

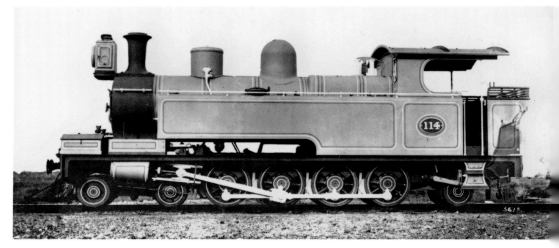

The first Class D 4-8-2T, designed by William Milne for Natal Government Railways, entered service in 1888. Later designated Class A by South African Railways, this successful type eventually numbered over a hundred locomotives, including No. 114 from Dübs of Glasgow in 1898. She later became SAR No. 187. (Alon Siton collection)

The original photograph was inscribed 'Driver Burrows, formerly of Newton Heath, Lancashire & Yorkshire Railway', who must have emigrated to South Africa from England. It was quite usual for experienced British railwaymen to relocate to the outposts of the Empire. His handsome locomotive is Orange Free State Railways 6th Class 4-6-0 No. 94, built by Sharp Stewart in 1898. (Alon Siton collection)

One of the earliest locomotives to carry a North British works plate was Central South African Railways Class 8C No. 479, built in 1903. The order for thirty such 4-8-0s had been placed with Neilson, but during their construction the merger took place with Sharp Stewart and Dübs, and the North British Locomotive Co. was born. (Alon Siton collection)

Of similarly American appearance to the 4-8-0 above, this Cape Government Railways 6th Class 4-6-0 was another Neilson order completed in 1903 under the NBL name. She was one of a pair of experimental engines, the first in South Africa to be superheated, later becoming Class 6L. (Alon Siton collection)

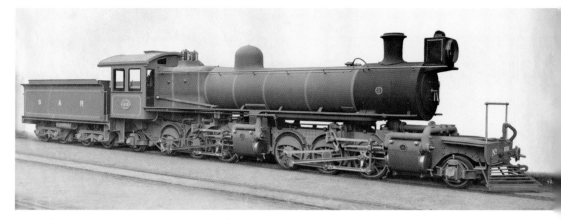

The Beyer Garratts were not the only articulated steam locomotives to grace Africa's railways. This impressive North British 2-6-6-2 was an experimental 'Mallet' type ordered by the newly nationalised South African Railways in 1910. Class ME No. 1618 was a success and, unusually for a 'one-off', she lasted twenty-five years in service. Five more followed, built to an enlarged design, also supplied by North British. (Alon Siton collection)

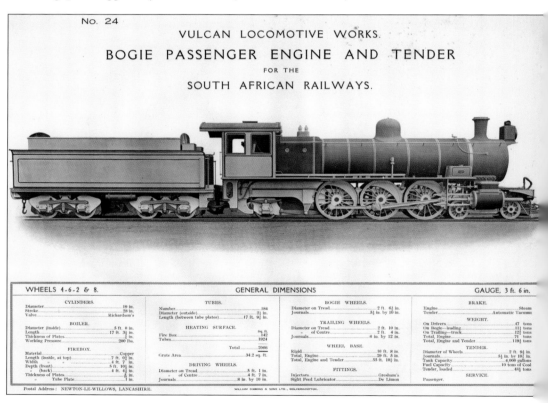

Of all of the names given to different wheel arrangements, the term 'Pacific' for a 4-6-2 is probably the most iconic. Vulcan Foundry built a batch of four Pacifics for South African Railways in 1912, Nos 780–783, of Class 5. They were an enlarged version of the Class 5B, and No. 781 survives in preservation at Bloemfontein. (Alon Siton collection)

While British Railways withdrew steam locomotives with indecent haste, after less than ten years of service in some cases, South African Railways certainly got its money's worth. Class 14R 4-8-2 No. 1581 was built by North British in 1914. She was modernised with a new boiler in 1950 and in this 1981 photo she was on hire to the National Railways of Zimbabwe due to a motive power shortage in the former Southern Rhodesia. (Alon Siton collection)

The steep, tightly curved line over South Africa's Hex River pass is more than 3,000 feet above sea level. In 1914 a troop train was on its way to Cape Town taking men of the Kaffrarian Rifles to sail for the Western Front. It is said that the driver had boasted how fast he could negotiate the pass. An obelisk carries the inscription 'Faithful Unto Death' with the names of the eight soldiers killed when the train derailed and plunged 30 feet down a slope. This photograph may show that train before the disaster. (Alon Siton collection)

Another of the numerous SAR Class 14R 4-8-2s, No. 1740 *MASONS HILL*, was photographed leaving the original, and soon to be closed, Durban station in 1980 with a special train to commemorate the centenary of the Durban to Pietermaritzburg line. The locomotive was built by Robert Stephenson's in 1915, and reboilered in the 1930s. (Alon Siton collection)

This dramatic photograph shows South African Railways Class 16C 4-6-2 No. 819, built in 1919, sending a column of black smoke skywards as she rounds a curve. Designed by D. A. Hendrie, she was one of thirty built by North British. They worked express passenger trains from Pretoria and Johannesburg, including the prestigious Natal mail. (Alon Siton collection)

This is a wonderful, evocative shot of a 16C, No. 824m accelerating past an elegant, lattice-post semaphore junction signal with a rake of vintage passenger stock. She was one of the second batch, built in 1921 by North British. Popular with their men, the 16Cs were good steamers, reliable, strong and fast. (Alon Siton collection)

South African Railways' Class 12 4-8-2 was also designed by Hendrie, for freight work. Forty-six were built in total, by North British and Beyer Peacock. One of the latter, No. 1863, built in Manchester in 1921, is shown in this official portrait. Thirty of the almost identical Class 12B followed from Baldwin in the USA. Both series were rebuilt with new boilers and reclassified 12R. (Alon Siton collection)

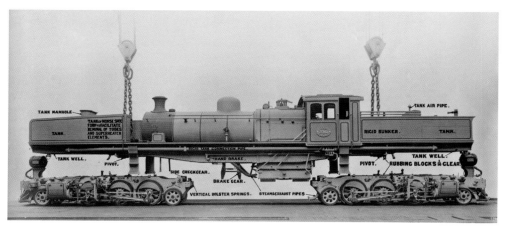

As well as the numerous Garratts and occasional Mallet, there was a third type of articulated locomotive operating in South Africa. This was 'Modified Fairlie' 2-6-2+2-6-2T No. 2310, built by North British in 1925. She lacks the separate fuel and water tanks of the Garratt type and instead consists of a long rigid frame on two pivoted power bogies. She was a North British response to the success of the Beyer Garratt. (Alon Siton collection)

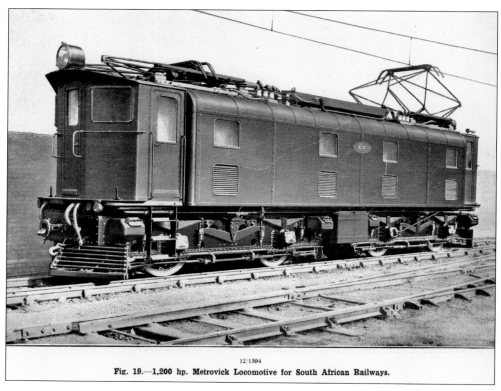

12/1594
Fig. 19.—1,200 hp. Metrovick Locomotive for South African Railways.

Electrification of South Africa's railways began in Natal in the 1920s, and once again it fell to British manufacturers to supply the equipment. The Manchester firm of Metropolitan Vickers was established in the field of electric traction, and this page from its 1939 catalogue depicts a SAR Class 1E electric locomotive of 1925. (Alon Siton collection)

South African Railways' Class GE Beyer Garratt 2-8-2+2-8-2T was designed with the lowest achievable axle loading for use on lightly laid permanent way. No. 2270 was built at Beyer Peacock's Gorton Foundry, Manchester, in 1926, one of a class of eighteen such locomotives. (Alon Siton collection)

An undated photograph, taken sometime after 1928, showing the official opening ceremony of a railway bridge over the Orange River. This is another example of a member of the locomotive crew being mentioned, the back of the print carrying an inscription by the driver, mentioning his fireman Rowe, who appears on the right of the image. (Alon Siton collection)

The first thirty-seven members of SAR's Class 15CA 4-8-2 were built in the USA and Italy. No. 2853, seen here in action, was one of the forty-seven that followed from North British in Glasgow in 1930. They were a redesign of the 15C Class, built by US firm Baldwin, after some of the American locomotives were sidelined with cracked frames. (Alon Siton collection)

The magnificent cast iron arch over the gates to the Hydepark works of the North British Locomotive Co., Glasgow, forms part of the background of this superb study. I wonder if it survives? The photograph shows the rotary cam valve gear of newly completed South African Railways Class 19C 4-8-2 No. 2460 in 1934. (Alon Siton collection)

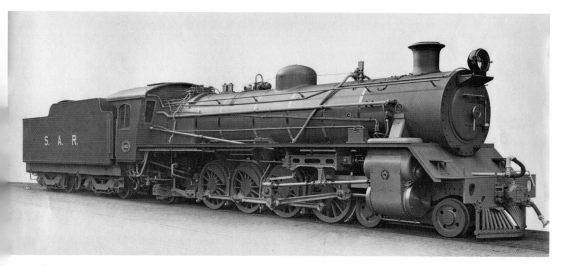

The 19Cs were versatile and lightweight locomotives used on main line and branch services. This 1935 North British workshop portrait shows SAR No. 2437, although her cab-side numberplate says 2462. One of them recorded a top speed of 67 mph – quite a feat for such a small-wheeled locomotive on 3-foot 6-inch gauge track! No. 2439 is preserved at Outeniqua Transport Museum. (Alon Siton collection)

The last 19C was North British works No. 24217. The very next locomotive on their list was No. 24218 of 1935, this was a 3-foot 6-inch gauge 2-6-2T for the African Explosives & Industries Ltd, a company founded in 1896 after gold was discovered at Witwatersrand. (Alon Siton collection)

Another industrial tank engine for South Africa, this time from Bagnall of Stafford, was this unusual 4-4-0T of 1936, for the 2-foot ½-inch gauge railway at the Natal Estates Ltd sugar plantation at Mount Edgecombe near Durban. Named *BURNSIDE*, note her spark-arresting chimney and unusually long rear overhang. (Alon Siton collection)

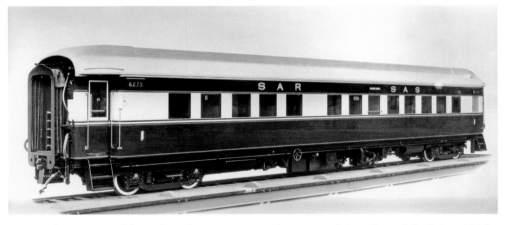

Designed to seat just fifteen first class passengers, this air-conditioned coach built in 1939 by Metropolitan Cammell of Birmingham must have been the last word in South African luxury travel. She was designed for the prestigious Blue Train, which had its roots in Cecil Rhode's dream of a Cape to Cairo route, but whose opulent rolling stock was destined never to reach beyond the south. (Alon Siton collection)

During the Second World War, Britain's workshops were occupied supplying munitions, but locomotive building continued, albeit in fewer numbers. This spectacular 1944 shot, taken at the Gorton Foundry shows South African Railways Class 15F 4-8-2 No. 2971. The first of this rakish-looking class had come from pre-war Germany, with Beyer Peacock contributing thirty. (Alon Siton collection)

The majority of the 255-strong 15F Class, however, were built by North British. This is South African Railways No. 3127 with sister engine No. 3099 double-heading a special train on the Pretoria to Pietersburg route in 1981. Both were built in Glasgow in 1947. (Alon Siton collection)

A visit to a British colliery in the last days of steam would reveal busy little 0-6-0 tanks being pushed to the limits of their capabilities. They didn't mess about with such small engines in South Africa. This colour transparency, taken at the Vryheid Coronation Colliery, north of Durban, shows North British 4-8-4Ts Nos 4 and 1, built 1948 and 1951 respectively, along with No. 5, a former SAR Class GEA 4-8-2+2-8-4T Beyer Garratt. (Alon Siton collection)

The railway from George to Knysna, midway along South Africa's beautiful southern coast, is known as the 'Outeniqua Choo Tjoe'. It was the last continuously steam-hauled passenger service in Africa until officially preserved in 1992. Ten years earlier, Class 24 2-8-4 No. 3627 *CITY OF GEORGE* was captured on film near Belvedere. She was built by North British in 1949. (Alon Siton collection)

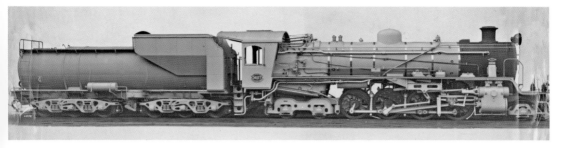

Sister engine No. 3607, also a 1949 product of North British, is the subject of this official portrait. The 2-8-4 wheel arrangement was unknown in Britain, but South African Railways took delivery of a hundred such Class 24 locomotives, with 4-foot 3-inch diameter driving wheels. (Alon Siton collection)

Another special train for the centenary of the Durban to Pietermaritzburg line in 1980 used a pair of beautifully prepared Garratts. SAR Class GMA/M 4-8-2+2-8-4Ts Nos 4066 and 4101 had additional water-carriers marshalled between them. Unusually, neither of them was a product of Beyer Peacock, No. 4066 coming from North British in 1953, and No. 4101 from Henschel of Germany in 1956. (Alon Siton collection)

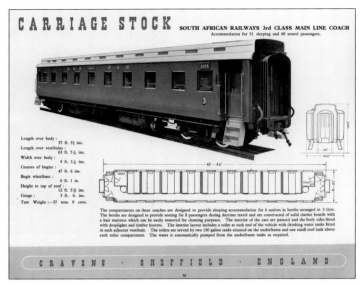

One of the UK rolling stock manufacturers that was prolific in the export market was Cravens of Sheffield. This third class coach from the firm's catalogue, dating from the 1950s, was designed with convertible compartments, each of which could sleep six 'natives', or seat eight. Contrast this with the Blue Train's first class accommodation, with fifteen passengers to the entire coach. (Alon Siton collection)

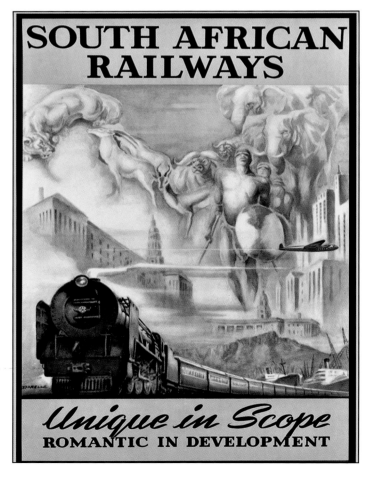

South African Railways' massive Class 25 4-8-4s were introduced from 1953, which dates this travel poster. 'Unique in Scope – Romantic in Development' is the message, with the powerful train superimposed against a strange vignette of African wildlife and native warriors with modern architecture and aircraft. (Alon Siton collection)

The giant Class 25s ran with Henschel patent condensing tenders. The first of the class was built in Germany and shipped to Glasgow, where the remaining eighty-eight locomotives were built by North British. This equipment significantly reduced water consumption, a vital requirement in South Africa's more arid regions. This official portrait shows SAR No. 3536, built by NBL in 1953. (Alon Siton collection)

The absence of buffers betrays the export status of this 0-4-0ST, named *HEX* and built in 1954 for South Africa's Electricity Supply Commission. The smart little engine was built at Robert Stephenson & Hawthorn's, Forth Street, Newcastle. This was the birthplace of *LOCOMOTION* and *ROCKET*, and 137 years of locomotive building there ended in 1960. (Alon Siton collection)

Tsumeb is a mining town in the former South West Africa, now Namibia, and in the late 1950s the local copper mining corporation ordered a batch of seven 2-foot gauge Garratt 2-6-2+2-6-2Ts. They were the last steam locomotives built by Beyer Peacock, and were similar to the SAR NGG16 Class, into which they were absorbed. This image shows No. TC11 outside the Gorton Foundry in 1958. (Alon Siton collection)

In 1960, British Prime Minister Harold Macmillan addressed the South African Parliament with his famous 'wind of change' speech. A year later the country became a republic. 1960 also saw the building of 135 of these handsome Class 5E1 electric locomotives at Metropolitan Vickers' works at Bowesfield in Stockton, County Durham. One of them is here being united with her bogies on a South African quayside. (Alon Siton collection)

Continuing clockwise, the next British possession we come to is Africa's most populous country, Nigeria. Gilbert Carter, Governor of Lagos, wanted a railway to exploit the country's resources and facilitate the movement of troops. Construction began in 1895, and this fascinating 1908 photograph shows Lagos Government Railways 0-6-0T No. 4 *IDDO*, built by Hunslet of Leeds in 1903. (Alon Siton collection)

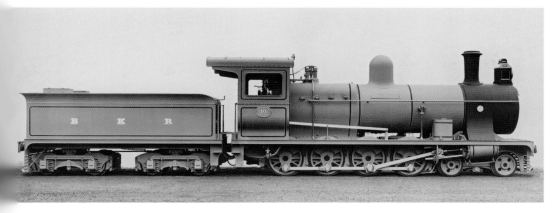

The Baro Kano Railway was an inland route in Nigeria, and in 1912, along with the aforementioned Lagos Government Railways, it was absorbed into the national Government Department of Railways. This rather oddly proportioned 4-8-0, No. 10 *EMIR OF BIDA,* was built for the BKR by North British in 1908. (Alon Siton collection)

Offa is a town in the west of Nigeria. This photograph was taken at the engine shed there and shows 4-6-0 No. 402, built by Nasmyth Wilson in Manchester in 1913. There were four of these locomotives and all were subsequently rebuilt as 4-6-4T engines. (Alon Siton collection)

The rebuilding took place in 1934/5 and resulted in a much more purposeful-looking locomotive. This is 4-6-4T No. 462, rebuilt from Nasmyth Wilson 4-6-0 No. 403, pausing with a goods train beside a water column. (Alon Siton collection)

Nasmyth Wilson also supplied Nigeria Railways with 4-8-0s for freight duties. No. 261 was built in 1914, and is seen here receiving some attention from one of her crew. The firm stopped building locomotives in the 1930s, and in 1940 the Ministry of Supply took over its Patricroft premises, which became a Royal Ordnance Factory. (Alon Siton collection)

Another fascinating vintage photograph showing a sister locomotive of No. 261. There were forty-four of these 4-8-0s built by Nasmyth Wilson, North British, and fellow Glasgow firm, William Beardmore. This one is in charge of a mixed freight and passenger train. A member of her crew seems to be in conversation with an onlooker as she stands in Offa, en route from Ibadan to Jebba. (Alon Siton collection)

The 133-mile Bauchi Light Railway was a 2-foot 6-inch gauge line in northern Nigeria, which opened in 1914 for the transport of tin from Jos to the main line at Zaria. This unusual 0-6-2, No. B57, was built by Kitson in Leeds in 1921. In this image, it appears she is about to receive some attention from the oil can. Sister engine, 1914-built No. 56, can be seen at the National Museum in Jos. (Alon Siton collection)

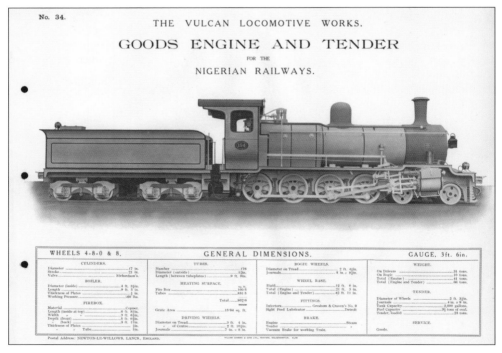

This page from the Vulcan Foundry catalogue shows the first of three 4-8-0s built for Nigerian Railways in 1922, No. 154. The Newton-le-Willows factory was established in 1830 by Charles Tayleur, and Robert Stephenson was an early partner. (Alon Siton collection)

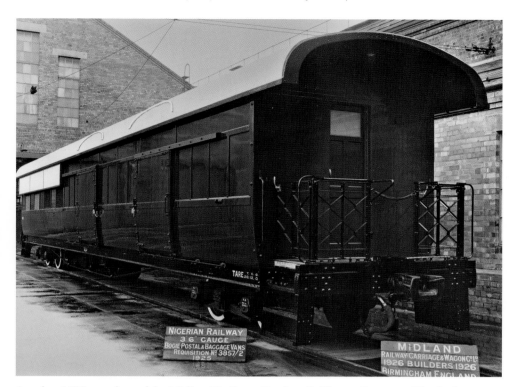

Another 1920s product of the Midland Railway Carriage & Wagon Company, Birmingham, was this postal and baggage van for Nigeria, built in 1926. There is passenger accommodation at the furthest end, with external shuttering for protection from the sun. Note the American-style end verandah. (Alon Siton collection)

D. W. 'Bill' Harvey was a British locomotive superintendent who spent four years working for Nigerian Railways before the Second World War. Fortunately for us, he took some photographs during his time there, including this one of 4-8-2 No. 729, the last of a series of five built by Armstrong Whitworth of Newcastle in 1928. (D. W. Harvey – Alon Siton collection)

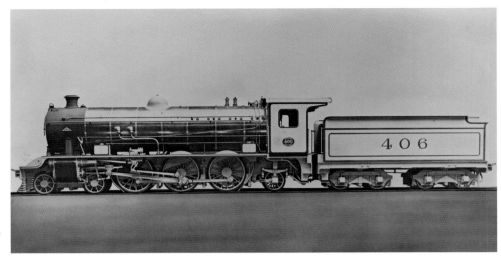

Nigerian Railway 4-6-2 No. 406 was the second of ten Class 405 Pacifics built between 1926 and 1928 by Nasmyth Wilson. They were used on passenger trains between Lagos and Kano, including the *North Mail* and the *Boat Express*. They were eventually replaced by diesels on the most important trains, but remained in service on lesser duties until the 1970s. (Alon Siton collection)

The 405s were given names such as No. 410 *MARY SLESSOR* after the Scottish missionary, or in the case of No. 412, seen here in another of Bill Harvey's photographs, *EMIR OF KAIAMA* – the title of a Nigerian chief. Later in their lives the locomotives gained smoke deflectors, although their efficacy is doubtful at the speeds that were attainable. (D. W. Harvey – Alon Siton collection)

W. G. BAGNALL, LTD. CASTLE ENGINE WORKS, STAFFORD

TYPE E. 2202. FOR LEADING DIMENSIONS SEE OTHER SIDE.

0-6-0 tank engines in the UK tended to be inside-cylindered, but on the narrower Cape Gauge used in Nigeria, outside cylinders and motion would be easier to maintain. This handsome locomotive, No. 18, was built by Bagnall of Stafford in 1928. Sister engine No. 5 survives at a museum at Enugu. (Alon Siton collection)

An official workshop portrait, taken outside the erecting shop at Vulcan Foundry shows Nigerian Railway 3-cylinder 2-8-2 No. 801 in photographic grey livery. She was built in 1928, the first of a class of five designed by T. Otway-Ruthven and named after Nigeria's colonial governor from 1919 to 1925, Sir Hugh Clifford. (Alon Siton collection)

Bill Harvey recorded this priceless image of seven proud Nigerian Railway employees inside an engine shed in the 1930s. They appear to be standing in front of one of the Bagnall 0-6-0T locomotives as she stands over an inspection pit. I wonder if any of the men received copies of the photograph at the time? (D. W. Harvey – Alon Siton collection)

Those men may have worked on everything from the Bagnall 0-6-0Ts to Nigeria's Beyer Garratts. 4-6-2+2-6-4T No. 513 carried the name *SIR JOHN MAYBIN* after Britain's Chief Secretary in Nigeria, who went on to become Governor of Northern Rhodesia. The locomotive was built by Beyer Peacock in 1939. (Alon Siton collection)

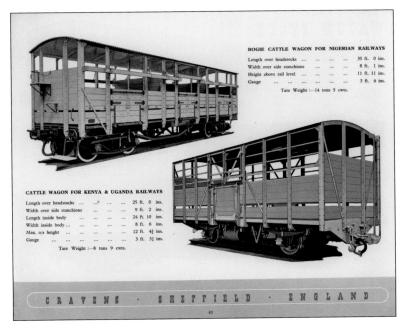

Earlier, we saw a South African sleeping car in the 1950s Cravens catalogue. As we can see, that company's vehicles carried a variety of payloads across Africa. This page shows two different cattle trucks, one for Nigeria and the other for the Kenya Uganda Railway, which by this time would have become part of EAR. (Alon Siton collection)

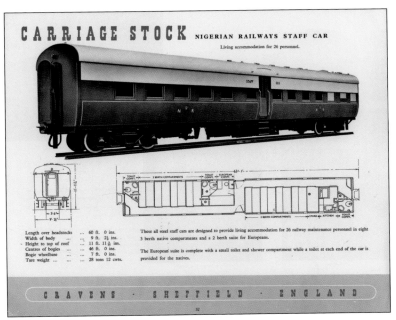

Yet another example of the shameless segregation that was prevalent across the British Empire, is the layout of this Nigerian Railways Staff Car, again from the Cravens catalogue. (Alon Siton collection)

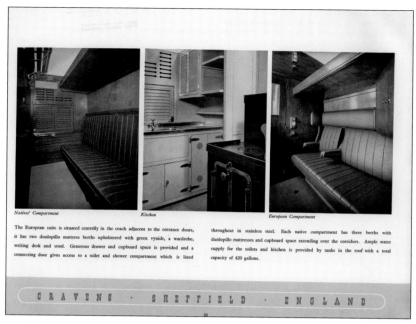

There was sleeping accommodation along with showers and toilets for twenty-six members of staff. While the spacious 'European' en-suite compartment slept two people, the 'natives' were expected to share toilets and showers, and sleep in smaller, three-bed compartments. (Alon Siton collection)

This is a 1959-built Gloucester Railway Carriage & Wagon bogie goods brake for Nigeria, featuring open and enclosed freight sections with a guard's compartment with lookout duckets. The following year, Nigeria gained independence from Britain and much of her railway equipment would be procured from other parts of the world. (Alon Siton collection)

Nigeria had a modern steam fleet by this time, with 2-8-2s such as No. 166 *RIVER WURKAM*, seen here in this depot scene. The 'Rivers' were built by North British in Glasgow from 1947, and were the basis for the EAR Tribal Class. Here, steam men look on suspiciously as a new German-built Maschinenbau Kiel diesel locomotive arrives for duty in August 1961. (Alon Siton collection)

Approximately 200 miles west of Nigeria was the British colony of Gold Coast, whose eastern region was for a time referred to as British Togoland. In 1921, four metre-gauge 4-6-0s were ordered from Nasmyth Wilson, and they became Togoland Railway Nos 40–43. They were similar to a standard design supplied by many manufacturers to the metre-gauge railways of India. (Alon Siton collection)

Showing to good effect the tumblehome cab-side profile that is characteristic of so many African steam locomotives, this is Gold Coast Railway 4-6-0 No. 184 *SIR MATTHEW NATHAN*. She was named after yet another colonial administrator, and was one of five built by Robert Stephenson's in 1924. (Alon Siton collection)

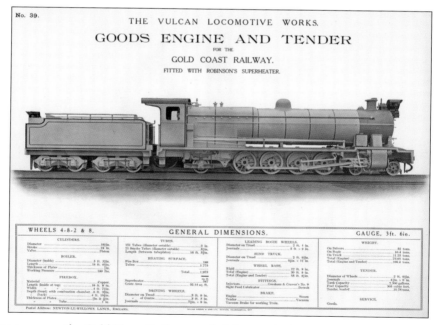

In the same year, the Gold Coast Railway took delivery of a batch of four 4-8-2s from Vulcan Foundry. They were given running numbers 221 to 224. Two further batches followed, also from Newton-le-Willows, in 1938 and 1949, bringing the class total to twenty-four. (Alon Siton collection)

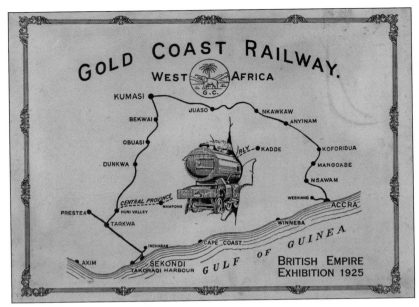

The Wembley Exhibition of 1924/5 showcased the rich cultural and industrial diversity of the British Empire. As well as iconic exhibits such as Gresley's *FLYING SCOTSMAN*, there was a wealth of eye-opening *tableaux* from all of the 'red bits' on the world map. This is the cover of the official Gold Coast Railway book, issued at the exhibition. (Alon Siton collection)

The exhibition's Gold Coast book depicted the charming Accra Central station. The station opened in 1910 but by the 1950s its single-track approach had become inadequate. Accra is now the capital of modern-day Ghana. (Alon Siton collection)

Unloading Cocoa in the station yard, Sekondi. A bag of Cocoa weighs 144 lbs.

— 31 —

The Wembley Exhibition included an African hut village where people from Nigeria, the Gold Coast and Sierra Leone demonstrated traditional crafts, as well as the growing of nuts, rubber, and one of West Africa's major cash crops, cocoa. This scene from the official book shows railway workers unloading 144 lb bags of cocoa at Sekondi. (Alon Siton collection)

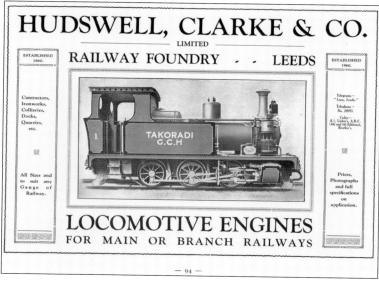

An advertisement in the exhibition book shows 0-6-0T No. 1 *TAKORADI*, built by Hudswell Clarke of Leeds. Incidentally, the contractor for Takoradi harbour was Robert McAlpine, who had also been involved in the Wembley Exhibition buildings. The first railway in the Gold Coast opened in 1903 from Takoradi inland to Tarkwa, a distance of 45 miles. (Alon Siton collection)

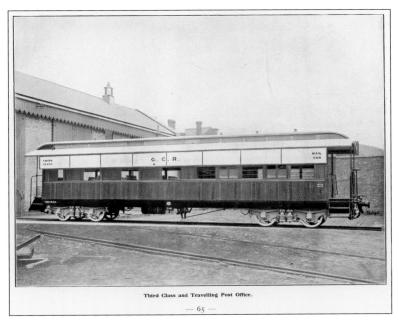

Third Class and Travelling Post Office.

— 65 —

Like many African railways, that in the Gold Coast was built to the Cape Gauge of 3 feet 6 inches. This clerestory-roofed combined third class coach and mail van was another product of the Gloucester Railway Carriage & Wagon Co. (Alon Siton collection)

A train being loaded with Manganese ore at Insuta.

— 50 —

Like most colonial lines, the raison d'être of the Gold Coast Railway was the extraction of the country's natural resources. This image from the exhibition book shows a train being loaded with manganese ore at Insuta (Nsuta). Notice the men pushing narrow-gauge trams along the top of the chutes. To this day, ore is taken by rail from here to Takoradi for export. (Alon Siton collection)

Locomotives of four classes, photographed in Tarkwa yard.

— 75 —

It is gold, not manganese, that is mined at Tarkwa. This scene shows at least eight employees of the Gold Coast Railway with members of four classes of locomotive in the yard. I wonder if those men knew they were going to appear in the Wembley Exhibition book? (Alon Siton collection)

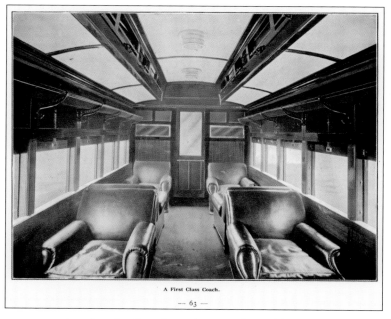

A First Class Coach.

— 63 —

This is the sumptuous interior of a first class saloon on the Gold Coast Railway. There was no cramming of eight people into a compartment here, with each passenger having his or her own individual armchair. (Alon Siton collection)

Passenger train en route from Kumasi to Accra.

— 57 —

Our final selection from the official Gold Coast Railway book depicts a passenger train en route from Kumasi to Accra, a journey of about 150 miles. Notice the number of passengers hanging out of the windows, presumably to keep cool as the train makes its way through the African jungle. (Alon Siton collection)

Between the wars, the British firms of Sentinel-Cammell and Clayton developed a series of geared steam railcars for use at home and abroad. They were more economical than conventional steam locomotives on lighter branch line duties. This photograph shows R.M.4, a twin unit for operation on the Gold Coast Railway, one of four built by Sentinel between 1927 and 1929. (Alon Siton collection)

The tricky business of transferring a 50-ton locomotive from ship to shore is in progress as a Hunslet-built 0-8-0T reaches the end of her voyage to the Gold Coast. A second locomotive can be seen on deck, awaiting lifting. One can only marvel at the ability of the crane operators and the men on the dockside to position the flanges of the locomotive's multiple wheels precisely between the rails. (Alon Siton collection)

Looking resplendent in her simple Gold Coast Railway livery, No. 12 is another of the same class. Twenty-four were built by Hunslet in Leeds between 1930 and 1953. They were very successful locomotives, and thirty-three more were built for Nigeria, of which at least two survive, albeit in derelict condition. (Alon Siton collection)

This vintage postcard shows a typical Gold Coast Railway passenger train that has stopped at a wayside station. The train is headed by 4-6-0 No. 187, built by North British in 1932. The locomotive appears to be of the same design as Stephenson-built *SIR MATTHEW NATHAN* of 1924. (Alon Siton collection)

Four Gold Coast Railway 4-8-2 locomotives of the 241 Class, built by Nasmyth Wilson in Manchester in 1936, await transfer to a cargo ship for Africa. The location is the Herculaneum Dock in Liverpool. The 30-mile road journey from Patricroft to the Mersey by low-loader must have been a slow one. (Alon Siton collection)

The Gold Coast Railway was another recipient of War Department locomotives, such as this Garratt 2-8-2+2-8-2T, No. 301. She was built by Beyer Peacock in Manchester in 1943, and others of the same design ran in Rhodesia, where they were known as the 18th Class. (Alon Siton collection)

This beautifully proportioned, lightweight 4-6-2, No. 261, was built by Beyer Peacock in 1948 for the Gold Coast Railway. She was built as a one-off to augment a pre-war batch of similar Pacifics. They were designed with a maximum axle weight of 12½ tons. Sadly, all main-line steam locomotives in what became Ghana were scrapped by the 1990s, and none survive in preservation. (Alon Siton collection)

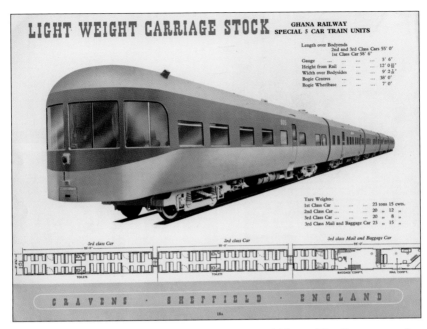

In 1957, the Gold Coast became the independent nation of Ghana. The Cravens catalogue from that time shows this impressive five-car lightweight rake, featuring an observation end to its first class buffet car. With integral steel and alloy construction, the set also included second and third class accommodation as well as mail-sorting facilities. (Alon Siton collection)

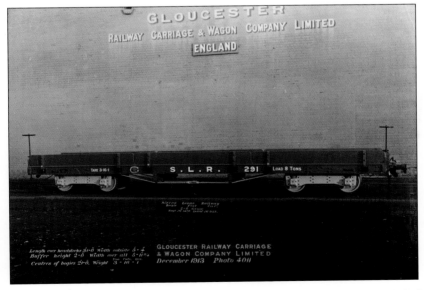

The westernmost railway in British Africa was in the tiny nation of Sierra Leone, Britain's first possession in Africa. This was a much smaller network than that found in the Gold Coast, and was built to the narrower gauge of 2 foot 6 inches. The Gloucester Railway Carriage & Wagon Co. supplied the Sierra Leone Railway with some bogie flat wagons in 1913, as seen here. (Alon Siton collection)

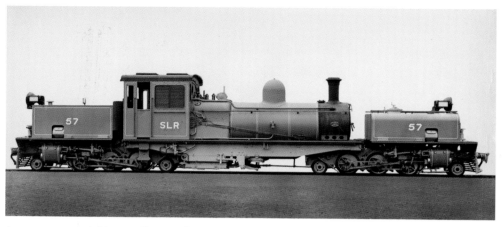

As on so many African railways, the Garratt became the mainstay of motive power in Sierra Leone. 2-6-2+2-6-2T No. 57 was built by Beyer Peacock in 1942, and would have had to cope with a huge wartime increase in rail traffic. However, competition from road transport would kill off the railways of Sierra Leone, which, apart from one serving the iron ore industry, all closed by 1974. (Alon Siton collection)

Some British-built locomotives have been repatriated from Africa for preservation, including some in working order. They include Beyer Peacock 1958-built South African NGG16 Garratt No. 138, which is ideal motive power for the twisting, steep and beautifully scenic Welsh Highland Railway from Porthmadog to Caernarfon. She is seen here at Waunfawr in May 2019. (Colin Alexander)